WOMEN OF THE BIG SKY

Women of the Big Sky

Liliana Ancalao

translated by

Seth Michelson

INTERNATIONAL EDITIONS
Barbara Goldberg, Series Editor

THE WORD WORKS
WASHINGTON, D.C.

The Word Works
P.O. Box 42164
Washington, D.C. 20015
editor@wordworksbooks.org

Cover image: Liliana Ancalao
Cover design: Susan Pearce Design
Author photograph: Morena Aimé Martínez
Translator photograph: Kevin Remington

ISBN: 978-1-944585-43-3

Acknowledgments

Grateful acknowledgment is made to the editors of the publications in which this poetry and prose first appeared: *Connotation Press, Latin American Literature Today, Washington Square Review*, and *World Literature Today*.

The translations were made possible by the generous support of a Translation Fellowship from the National Endowment for the Arts.

Thank you also to Washington and Lee University, including the Dean's Office, Provost's Office, Romance Languages Department, Latin American and Caribbean Studies Program, and the Center for Poetic Research.

A bow of gratitude and admiration is due to everyone at The Word Works.

Special, deep thanks are due to Nancy White and Barbara Goldberg for their visionary realization of this book within their phenomenal catalogue.

This book is dedicated to the Mapuche, and to indigenous peoples everywhere, in their struggles to reclaim their languages, rituals, practices, historicities, communities, cosmovisions, and lands. Mañumüwiñ ka pewkayal!

Contents

Preface

About 500 years ago, Liliana Ancalao's people, the Mapuche, were dispossesssed from their indigenous lands. They had lived there, hunted there, created art there for thousands of years. But Argentina, with its rapacious hunger for those same lands and the cheap labor the indigenous inhabitants represented, swallowed them whole.

For contemporary urbanites, it's hard to imagine that wrenching experience of rupture —that the relationship to the land represented the essence of its people. As Ancalao says, "The groundwork of memory surges from the land." In Ancalaeo's case, the trauma is felt at the gut level. Despite living an urban life today, Ancalao hungers for the intimacy of her community and "mother tongue," *Mapuzungan*, with its unique structure of "we" rather than "I." It was also the language spoken on the long road to exile during the genocidal divvying up of men, women, and children as slaves: "The clandestine whisper in the concentration camps. The language of solace among prisoners of war," as Ancalao writes. The great grandparents of her generation were sent to reservations and state schools, and learned to speak Spanish by force. However, Ancalao's own grandfather remembered the language all too well, could even speak it.

Ancestral memories stay fresh. Feeling displaced and uprooted leads to anger, grief, and the struggle for reclamation, to become centered and whole. Thus, her search for a place of stillness:

> I sense the need to push on who knows
> how far to conquer my fear of getting near
> them [native llamas] to measure myself in the deep space
> of their eyes and accept the miracle of a
> silence of snow.

And again, "If I can hold out they might allow me to / submerge myself in their eyes in their eyes infinite little / ones to stake myself for an instance in the / center of time..."

But perhaps she is wasting her time. Perhaps her desire to heal the painful rift from her native land and culture is useless. "I failed to find life's / secret because I went after / ghosts chasing stories and / spiders and jugs and leaves." Sometimes, she thinks of herself as small and helpless: "When I die I should cross the river but / what dog will guide me as I have / none: a skinny dog that smells my / cowardice will walk by my side."

Her work is replete with images of growing up unfettered, "to be freedom to be tenderness galloping with them loosed up on the land is a *trutuka* [trumpet] and we'll go galloping to cut loose the stars from the river—the circular movement I'll know at once what it is to be a warrior running freely toward/ death what visions burn in him."

Here the language is visceral—of the body, the skin, and never a doubt that the sensibility is feminine: "As girls loosed through the patio / and the sun gallops after us till the implacable / moon hits us with her tides..." And the fierce cold described so vividly in Seth Michelson's lyrical translation:

> As a girl in overalls I learned the cold was
> dark when my father's rambler classic
> wouldn't start meaning we'd walk to school
> cutting through weather fangs biting into
> our scant flesh I was two knees that ached
> we'd say what cold to see the vapor of our
> breath and have company.

Ancalao's poetry lives in multiple dimensions of time. Despite being a poetry of dispossession and loss, it is also mythic and archtypical, for the ages—the moon, the snow, the cold. Ancalao feels it her sacred duty to keep Mapuche heritage and language alive. To gift them to posterity, she must become ever more fluent in her ancestral tongue. For more than a century the Mapuzungun language represented banishment, assigned by the state as a mark of inferiority. But for Ancalao, it is a source of pride. She wants to reclaim and revitalize the language, to feel at home in it—not just for herself, but for all her people.

—Barbara Goldberg
Chevy Chase, Maryland

Liliana Ancalao and the Poetry of Puel Mapu

Etymologically, the word Mapuche blends the Mapuzungun word "mapu," meaning "land," with "che," meaning "people." In other words, the Mapuche self-identify as "the people of the land." Moreover, the preposition in that adjective phrase is itself of special importance. That is, the Mapuche understand themselves as being people *of* the land, and not its possessors, owners, or privatizers, for example. Rather, as archaeological records attest in concert with longstanding Mapuche oral histories, their culture emerged more than 19,000 years ago from a nomadic people traversing the southern third of what is today mapped most commonly as continental South America. For most of that time, the Mapuche moved freely across the land, ranging from central and southern Chile to central and southern Argentina. Across that expanse, they practiced regionally variable but overlapping cosmovisions, all the while engaging in seasonal modes of hunting and gathering, creating pottery and statuary, and flourishing in the region.

However, in 1520 the vibrant mosaic of indigenous life in the region would be profoundly altered. This was the year of the arrival of Europeans, beginning with the Portuguese explorer Fernão de Magalhães (1480-1521), who is perhaps better known in the Anglophone world as Ferdinand Magellan. His arrival marks the beginning of a five-century onslaught against the indigenous peoples of the region that continues to this day. That onslaught has consistently combined the usurpation of indigenous land with the murder of its peoples, with the Europeans thereby devastating not only the Mapuche, but also the Kawésqar, Aónikenk-Tehuelche, Huarpes, Huilliche, Puelche, Selk'nam, Teushen, and Yagán, among many others. This politics of displacement, dehumanization, and assassination culminated in the early nineteenth century in the formation of the modern nation-states of Chile and Argentina, wherein it remains active to this day, with recent examples including the murders of Camilo Catrillanca in Chile and Rafael Nahuel in Argentina, as well as the murder in Argentina of Santiago Maldonado, an activist for indigenous land rights.

From this complex history, from this bloodied *mapu*, comes the contemporary Mapuche poet Liliana Ancalao. She was born in 1961 in Diadema Argentina, in the southern Argentine province of Chubut, where Ancalao's great-grandparents had been forcibly relocated during the so-called "Conquest of the Desert," a genocidal landgrab by the Argentine government in the last quarter of the nineteenth century. Consequently,

Ancalao's grandparents, like all Mapuche children on reservations, were forced to learn and converse in Spanish in the state school. This marked an especially sinister and devastating form of coloniality of power: The state aimed to erase Mapuche life and culture through the systematic repression and replacement of its language.

The impact of this linguistic violence resounds to this day, with Ancalao's reclamation of Mapuzungun in her writing being one example of an important contemporary contestation of it. More broadly, as alluded to earlier, the late nineteenth and early twentieth-century assault on Mapuzungun and on Mapuche life also included the reorganization of rural life by the state, much to the detriment of Mapuche autonomy and wellbeing. As a result, Ancalao's parents, like many Mapuche, found themselves compelled to migrate to the city in search of work. This accounts for Ancalao's relatively urban upbringing compared to millennia of her Mapuche ancestors. Today, from her home in the Patagonian city of Comodoro Rivadavia, in Chubut, she addresses precisely such ruptures, writing often in her poetry and prose with eloquence, precision, urgency, and clarity of the historical displacement, linguistic censorship, and material violence suffered by the Mapuche. She similarly undertakes such work as an important oral historian of her people.

Through those intertwined cultural practices, Ancalao strives to reclaim her Mapuche identity from centuries of attempts by both church and state to deform, destabilize, discredit, and erase it. That is, in a rediscovered Mapuzungun, Ancalao's writing bears witness to the endurance and resurgence of her people against a diversity of violence. It is her testament to Mapuche power, pride, poise, resilience, and beauty, and it comes only after decades of study of Mapuzungun under multiple teachers. Accordingly her voice is as crucial as it is compelling to listen to, both transhistorically and currently. After all, Ancalao is working to rescue and put into circulation the imperiled stories, cosmovision, music, history, mythos, and *mapu* of her people, and this helps to complicate and influence transnational conversations about such crucial (and mutually ensnarled) topics as racism, sexism, poverty, and pollution, to name but a few.

Importantly, too, such work begins for Ancalao in language, meaning in Mapuzungun. Ancalao is poignantly aware of the oral linguistic tradition of Mapuzungun; there was no written system for it prior to Conquest, and no definitive codification exists to date. Thus, to a certain extent, in writing poetry in Mapuzungun, Ancalao is both reinvigorating a besieged language by breathing it into the present poetically, *and* performing a subversive poetic intervention by defiantly usurping the weapon of written literacy and wielding it

critically against its hegemonic oppressor, Spanish-language literacy. Moreover, in her writing in Mapuzungun, she is creating new possibilities for rememorating, articulating, and conceiving life, both Mapuche and otherwise. Simultaneously, too, she is striving to help to restore a cultural continuum long predating Conquest. And whenever she speaks, translates, or listens to Mapuzungun, she also is embodying a living ancient history. Thusly empowered, and working in multiple temporalities at once, she pores over historical records, anthropological texts, literature, music, and global cultural production by and about indigenous people, and all of this feeds her writing life, whether in her poetry, historiography, oral histories, or advocacy of her people.

It bears mention, too, that Ancalao also practices a powerful form of collaborative Mapuche politics. This is evident, for example, in her participation in the communitarian creation in 1994 of Ñankulawen, a group of Mapuche in Comodoro Rivadavia working together to explore the past, to support one another in the present, and to carry Mapuche life soundly into the future. In other words, Ñankulawen serves as an invaluable cultural nexus for Mapuche, both in the region and beyond. Furthermore, such centers are as necessary now as ever to the independence and vitality of the 1.7 million Mapuche living in Chile and Argentina. For they are everywhere menaced by the nation-states mapped over their *mapu*, with current crises including large-scale pollution by national and multinational industries, continued population displacements, severe deforestation, significant pay gaps for Mapuche in the labor force, systematic educational inequality for Mapuche, unequal access to and protections by federal and local law for Mapuche, and even the outright murder with impunity of Mapuche people and their allies, such as the recent cases of Rafael Nahuel and Santiago Maldonado, for example.

Through and against such saturating violence, Ancalao raises her voice. She sings a poetry that is by turns trenchant and mellifluous, urgent and timeless. Moreover, she sings not only of the historical brutalities and humiliations perpetrated against her people, but also of their courage, beauty, strength, and complexity. She celebrates their resilience and creativity. She shares their insights into ecological, sociopolitical, and spiritual wellbeing. She critiques the state while also imaging it otherwise. And she examines the potential of Mapuche life to transform the world for the better for everyone.

In short, then, Ancalao is a poet whom we all need. She is teaching us to reclaim our language(s) with tenderness, hope, and precision, and to respect those of others. She is teaching us to listen to one another with rapt attention, patience, and compassion. She

is exemplifying ways to be courageous and self-effacing, whether in excavating historical atrocities or in theorizing new conceptions of who we are and who we could be. For through the tropes and figures of poetry, and through her reclamation of Mapuzungun, Ancalao is creating for us new modes of looking into the past, understanding the present, and imagining better futures. Thusly her voice announces both individual and collective possibilities for creating the conditions for more informed and harmonious ways of sharing our precious time together on this Earth, this *mapu*.

For these reasons and more, and however paradoxically, Ancalao as artist is bravely plunging deeply inward and backward so as to turn outward and forward to you in conversation. In other words, through her poetry, for example, she is opening a Mapuche worldview to a new kind of witnessing. She is eliciting a new and hybrid mode of collaboration with a transcultural, multilingual readership, and this in turn encourages us to re-envision our worlds via a careful attention to the potentiality of language(s) to make possible new ways of being. Accordingly you will encounter her texts herein in Mapuzungun, Spanish, and English; your struggle with and between them is an instantiation of the lived struggle of our shared postcolonial reality. Put differently, this is Ancalao intimating to us her deepest hopes for humankind to form more inclusive, pacifistic, and egalitarian communities of difference. And this is clear throughout her written oeuvre, wherein she works tirelessly to create space in the body politic not only for the Mapuche, but also for all Mapuche, not to mention all indigenous peoples, women, migrants, and so many other overlooked, minoritized, and/or silenced groups and peoples threatened with erasure by the state.

So please accept Ancalao's invitation here, dear reader. Please join her in poetically recognizing how we might listen to one another with more concentration, openness, and compassion. See Ancalao tracing new and crucial pathways towards more pacifistic futures. Hear her praising the nourishing potentiality of a politics of inclusion based in radical listening. Through such a reorientation you might come to understand the phenomenology of her finest poetry, which leads us to understand how she somehow lives both "seeing herself [as] a ruins on the map of dreams" *and* as the "impossible flowers" enduring in the landscape. Such is our charge, she suggests: to learn to carry the sorrows of the *mapu* while also being living extensions of its capacity for eruptions of ravishing, inexplicable beauty.

—*Seth Michelson*
Lexington, Virginia

WOMEN OF THE BIG SKY

La memoria de la tierra sagrada

Con inmensa responsabilidad traigo acá estas palabras, como ser humano de este planeta, como mujer, como parte del pueblo mapuche, un pueblo que después de una hecatombe, viene juntando lentamente sus pedazos.

Soy de acá, del sur, del principio de mi mundo, lugar al que hoy llaman patagonia, lugar al que hoy publicitan turísticamente como fin del mundo.

Vivo en Comodoro Rivadavia.

A esta ciudad llegaron, muy jóvenes mi papá Ancalao y mi mamá Meli, quienes debieron dejar el campo, corridos por la pobreza material. Debieron abandonar un espacio limitado y asignado por el estado argentino, después de la Guerra del desierto. Debieron dejar el campo porque no era suficiente para dar sustento a todos, cambiar el ciclo de la siembra y el ciclo de las pariciones, por un empleo, un salario, horarios y patrones.

De este hermoso par, nacimos seis hijos. Cuando nací en 1961, mi familia estaba instalada en un campamento petrolero. En aquel momento la empresa que administraba la extracción de este combustible fósil era holandesa. Mi papá fue obrero petrolero durante 30 de sus años y mi mamá fue empleada doméstica de los administradores de la empresa.

Nosotros como niños, pasamos jugando sobre puentes de metal debajo de los cuales corrían arroyitos de agua, aceite y petróleo. Pisamos la tierra negra de petróleo alrededor de los pozos abandonados. Nosotros, los desmemoriados.

Hoy, la cuenca del Golfo San Jorge, en la que se encuentra la ciudad de Comodoro Rivadavia, sigue siendo un lugar de explotación petrolera, se extrae petróleo del suelo y también de la plataforma submarina.

Hoy, a los habitantes de la ciudad nos controlan el consumo de agua y periódicamente cortan el suministro a los distintos barrios, hasta que se vuelven a llenar las reservas. Las administradoras del recurso justifican los cortes de agua con la rotura de las cañerías

Memory of the Sacred Land

With tremendous responsibility I share here these words, as a human being on this planet, as a woman, as part of the Mapuche people, a people who after a massacre, are coming together slowly after being shattered.

I'm from here, the South, the beginning of the world, a place that today is called Patagonia, a place that today is publicized touristically as the end of the world.

I live in Comodoro Rivadavia.

Very young, my father, Ancalao, and my mother, Meli, arrived at this city, forced from the countryside, run off by material poverty. They were forced to abandon a limited space assigned by the Argentine state after the War of the Desert. They were forced off that land because it was insufficient to sustain everyone, forced to swap the time of sowing and of calving for a job, salary, schedule, and bosses.

From that beautiful couple we six children were born. When I was born in 1961, my family had settled in an oil camp. In that moment the company that oversaw the mining of that fossil fuel was Dutch. My father was an oil worker for 30 years and my mother was a housekeeper for administrators of the company.

As children we spent our days playing on metal bridges beneath which flowed little rivers of water, oil, and petroleum. We walked through blackened earth around abandoned wells. We, the forgetful.

Today, the basin of the Gulf of San Jorge, in which is situated the city of Comodoro Rivadavia, continues to be a site of oil exploitation, with oil extracted from the ground and from an undersea platform.

Today, they control our use of water and they periodically cut the supply to certain neighborhoods, until the reserves are restored. The administrators of the natural resource justify the water cuts by blaming them on breaks in the pipelines, but we all think

que transportan el agua desde los lagos, pero todos sospechamos que son las empresas petroleras que operan en la zona las que utilizan el agua en cantidades exorbitantes para extraer el petróleo.

Y estamos entrampados, aún, los que no necesitamos trabajar para las petroleras, testigos de la depredación de la tierra y muchos, siendo parte, mes a mes, año a año, por un salario, una obra social, una jubilación.

Es la trampa del capitalismo.

En el sur de este continente, nació mi historia, el relato de mi pueblo Mapuche.

En mi historia hay un antes y un después de lo que los más ancianos recuerdan como el tiempo "cuando se perdió el mundo", un antes y un después de lo que historiadores occidentales llaman "conquista del desierto y pacificación de la Araucanía", aproximadamente en el año 1880 del calendario gregoriano.

Un antes y un después del momento en que la primera bala del Winchester trizó el universo. El rifle que el capitalismo compró al ejército chileno-argentino para que nos eliminara.

Tuvieron que matarnos para clavar sus garras deforestadoras, desertificantes, depredadoras, contaminantes; sus garras civilizadas, en el wall Mapu, el territorio. Y nos mataron de diferentes modos: a balazos, desangrados, hambreados, separándonos de nuestros hijos, borrándonos la memoria.

Ahí, cuando se perdió el mundo. Cuando pisotearon la tierra. Cuando destruyeron el puente de la cordillera con fronteras, cuando los latifundios clavaron los postes del alambre y parcelaron el territorio. Hace poco más de un siglo. Silenciaron nuestro idioma, desarmaron nuestra organización política, desmembraron nuestros lazos amorosos, desparramaron a nuestros parientes, delimitaron nuestros espacios, trajeron una religión y una educación ajenas a la naturaleza.

Nuestra historia ha estado siempre, espiritualmente, ligada a la tierra. Nuestra relación con la tierra no es sólo de extracción para recoger sus frutos y cosechas, sino de veneración.

it's due to the oil companies in the region using exorbitant amounts of water to mine oil.

And we're all caught in this, those of us who don't need to work for the oil companies, and the many who do, playing a part month after month, year after year, for income, social security, retirement, all of us witnesses to the plunder of the earth.

It's the trap of capitalism.

In the south of this continent, my history was born, the history of the Mapuche people.

In my history there's a before and an after to the time that the eldest remember as "the loss of the world," a before and an after to what western historians call "the Conquest of the Desert, and the pacification of Auracanía," in approximately 1880 of the Gregorian calendar.

A before and after to the moment in which the first bullet from a Winchester smashed through the universe. That rifle that capitalism purchased for the Chilean-Argentine army to try to eliminate us.

They had to kill us to sink their deforesting, desertifying, predatory, contaminating talons, their civilizing talons, into wall mapu, our land. And they killed us in many ways: by shoooting us, by bleeding us out, starving us, separating us from our children, erasing our memory.

That moment, when the world was lost. When they trampled the land. When they destroyed the bridge of the mountains with borders, when the plantations sank their posts of wired fence and carved up the land. Little more than a century ago. They silenced our language, undid our political organization, dismembered our amorous unions, scattered our relatives, delimited our spaces, brought a religion and an education oblivious to nature.

Our history has always been tied spiritually to nature. Our relation to nature is not only one of extraction to collect its fruits, but also one of veneration. We renew ourselves

Cíclicamente nos renovamos con sus fuerzas. Las fuerzas de la tierra a las que respetamos y a las que hacemos propicias cumpliendo con nuestros rituales.

Nuestra historia ha estado siempre, resistentemente, ligada a la historia del planeta. Nuestra memoria oral recuerda los relatos de inundaciones, erupciones volcánicas y terremotos que dieron vuelta el espacio, lo sacudieron hasta hacernos pensar que era nuestro fin. Y la realización del ritual, el ngillatun, ese tiempo- espacio adonde ofrendamos y pedimos, nos volvió a acomodar en el ciclo de la vida.

Pero el cataclismo de la guerra y la depredación de la tierra no pertenecen a la historia del planeta sino a la historia de la humanidad. Esta muerte desembarcó aquí con el winka, con su cosmovisión, que considera al hombre como el rey del planeta, que considera que el río, el pájaro y el aire, existen para estar a su servicio, que considera a la tierra como un recurso económico.

Hoy, todos sabemos, que esta agonía que lleva poco más de un siglo en el sur, se inició mucho antes en el resto del planeta. Sabemos también que la destrucción se ha acelerado en el último siglo. En el siglo pasado, siglo del vértigo, en el que nacimos los aquí presentes.

En la historia de mi pueblo yo nací dos generaciones después de la guerra del desierto. Nosotros, los Ancalao Meli, como muchos otros niños mapuche nacidos en la ciudad, éramos inconcientes del dolor de la tierra, no sabíamos quiénes éramos, de qué pueblo, qué raíces, qué historia. El estado se había ocupado de borrarnos la memoria. Ésa había sido parte de su política de integración.

Nacimos en el tiempo de la desmemoria. Fuimos niños y adolescentes sin memoria. Esta desmemoria conveniente a los estados nacidos de la matanza y el robo, conveniente también a las dictaduras militares.

El año 1992, cuando se cumplieron los quinientos años del desencuentro, marcó un hito en nuestra conciencia y aquellos que nos veníamos cuestionando nuestra identidad, comenzamos a actuar para recuperar la memoria.

Y la memoria nos sigue trayendo respuestas que iluminan.

cyclically with its power. Power that we respect and encourage by practicing our rituals.

Our history has always been tied resiliently to the history of the planet. Our oral memory remembers accounts of floods, volcanic eruptions, and earthquakes that flipped space, shaking it enough to make us think it was our end. And the practice of our rituals, the ngillatun, that space- time to which we made offerings and supplications, returned us to the cycle of life.

The cataclysm of war and the depredation of the land belong not to the history of the planet, but to the history of humanity. That death was spawned here with the winka, with their cosmovision that considers man the king of the planet; that considers rivers, birds, and air to exist in servitude; that considers the land an economic resource.

Today we all know that agony that began little more than a century ago in the Souther began much earlier in the rest of the world. We know, too, that the destruction accelerated in the previous century. In the previous century, century of vertigo, in which we here and present were born.

In the history of my people, I was born two generations after the War of the Desert. We, the Ancalao Meli, like so many other Mapuche children born in the city, we're unaware of the agony of the land, we didn't know who we were, from what people, what roots, what history. The state had been busy erasing our memory. This had been part of their plan for integration.

We were born in the time of amnesia. We were young children and teens without memory. That amnesia so convenient to states born of slaughter and robbery, and convenient to military dictatorships, too.

The year 1992, which signaled five-hundred years since the failed encounter, marked a milestone in our awareness, and those of us questioning our identity began to act to reclaim our memory.

And memory continues to bring us illuminating answers.

Ahora sé que soy mapuche, que mapuche significa ser humano de la tierra.

Ahora sé que el idioma que nació de mi pueblo, allí, en el principio del mundo y desde el principio del mundo es el mapudungun, que significa el idioma de la Tierra.

Ahora sé, que el kultrún, nuestro instrumento sagrado, representa al planeta, a wenu Mapu que es el espacio de la atmósfera, a trufken Mapu que es la superficie y a minche Mapu que es el subsuelo. Que en el kultrún se representan los cuatro ciclos de las estaciones a partir del Wiñoy Tripantu, el año nuevo que en nuestro hemisferio sur es en el mes de junio.

Ahora que las fuerzas de la naturaleza están cortadas por alambrados, cables y caños.

Minche Mapu entubada
Trufken Mapu habitada por herejes
Wenu Mapu sofocada por gases.
Ahora que al planeta le niegan su condición de sacro.

↳ sagrado

Este relato de la historia del pueblo mapuche, nos encuentra en este milenio, haciendo circular, nuevamente, la memoria.

La memoria de los pueblos debe regresar hasta esa etapa en que la Tierra era sagrada, para recuperar sus rituales y restaurar nuestra fuerza. La fuerza que necesitamos para hacer frente a sus depredadores.

Porque aquella vez no se perdió el mundo.

Mientras Francisco Pascasio Moreno, prócer de los naturalistas argentinos, organizaba la exhibición de nuestros esqueletos en las vitrinas del museo natural de la ciudad de La Plata; mientras el mismo donaba con generosidad 7.500 has de nuestro territorio al estado argentino, para la creación de un área protegida como Parque Nacional, mientras los winkas pensaban cómo proteger a la naturaleza de sí mismos; algunos de sus prisioneros de guerra pudieron huir.

Huyeron de las ciudades, de las casas de los ricos, adonde se los había entregado como esclavos, de los campos de concentración, de los campos con propietarios; y rumbearon al lugar en el que habían estado sus comunidades.

I now know I'm Mapuche, that Mapuche means person of the land.

I now know that the language that was born of my people, there at beginning of the world and since the beginning of the world is Mapudungun, which means language of the Land.

I now know that the kultrún, our sacred instrument, represents the planet, the wenu Mapu that is the atmosphere, and the trufken Mapu that is the surface, and the minche Mapu that is the underground. That on the kultrún are represented the four cycles of the seasons since the Wiñoy Tripantu, the new year in our southern hemisphere in the month of June.

Now the forces of nature are cut by wire fences, cables, and ducts.

Minche Mapu run through with tubes
Trufken Mapu peopled by brutes
Wenu Mapu suffocated by gas
Now that they deny the planet is sacred.

This version of the history of the Mapuche people reaches us in this millenium, stirring memory to circulate anew.

Peoples' memory should return to that stage in which the Land was sacred so as to recuperate their rituals and restore our power. The power that we need to face their predators.

Because that time the world wasn't lost.

While Francisco Pascasio Moreno, hero of the Argentine naturalists, was organizing the exhibition of our skeletons in glass displays in the Natural Museum in the city of La Plata; while he was generously donating 7,500 hectares of our land to the Argentine state for the creation of a protected area like a National Park; while the winkas were wondering how to defend nature from themselves; some of their prisoners of war were able to escape.

They fled from cities, from the houses of the wealthy where they'd been handed over like slaves, from concentration camps, from countryside with owners, and made their way back to the places where their communities had once been.

Los relatos que vamos recuperando, ahora, nos iluminan.

Siempre, hay un anciano que cuenta lo que quedó en la memoria de la familia: un hombre, o una mujer, a veces un niño, perdido en la inmensidad de un paisaje desconocido. Un ser humano hambriento, sediento, cansado, que quiere volver a reunirse con sus seres amados, comienza a sentir que no podrá con su cuerpo.

Entonces aparece un nahuel, el tigre... o un pangue, el puma, a veces un pájaro, el ñanco. Un newen, una fuerza de la naturaleza, compasivo. Que guía al extraviado, que escucha sus palabras de dolor, le trae alimento, le señala las aguadas, lo acompaña hasta que está a salvo.

Y allí en el medio del agradecimiento del ser humano de la tierra, surge el taüll el canto sagrado de esa fuerza propicia, el taüll atesorado que nos recuerda que la Mapu nos siguió reconociendo, después del cataclismo de la guerra.

Hace poco tiempo, escuché el canto del bosque en la voz de un machi muy joven. Un canto profundo y hermoso, que acariciaba el estómago. Estábamos todos muy conmovidos respirando ese momento sagrado, al lado de un río, Kurru leufu. Y la voz del machi se quebró y comenzó a llorar y el canto del bosque era un llanto: grave y sombrío.

En ese momento se depositó en mí, esta conciencia espiritual de la naturaleza, esta conciencia de ser parte de un tejido delicado, poderoso y ahora, dañado.

Mientras preparo estas palabras recuerdo, emocionada, que mañana, nos juntaremos como desde hace algunos sábados, en un barrio de la ciudad, a cantar.

A aprender canciones del vivir cotidiano. A aprender las canciones sagradas correspondientes a nuestro linaje. Las canciones para venerar a las fuerzas de la tierra, a sus newenes.

Seguiremos recuperando la memoria:

fill Mapu kiñekisungey ka inchiñ ka tüfa püllungey,
toda la tierra es una sola alma y somos parte de ella.

The stories we're now recovering illuminate us.

There's always an elder to share what remained in his memory of his family: a man, or a woman, sometimes a child, lost in the immensity of an unknown landscape. A hungry, thirsty, tired human being who wants to go back, reunite with his loved ones, but begins to feel he never will because of his body.

Then a nahuel, a tiger, appears...or a pangue, a puma, sometimes a bird, the ñanco. A newen, a natural power, compassionate. Who guides the lost, who listens to his words of pain, brings him food, leads him to water, accompanies him til he's safe.

And there, in the midst of the human being's gratitude for the land, emerges the taüll, the sacred song of that auspicious power, the treasured taüll that reminds us that the Mapu stayed with us, even after the cataclysm of war.

Not too long ago I heard the song of the forest in the voice of a very young machi. A deep and beautiful song that caressed the belly. We were all very moved by breathing that sacred moment, beside a river, Kurru leufu. And the voice of the machi broke and began to cry and the cong of the forest was a weeping: grave and somber.

In that moment a spiritual awareness of nature embedded itself in me, an awareness of being part of a delicate, powerful, and now damaged fabric.

As I prepare these words I remember, touched, that tomorrow we'll gather as we have for several Saturdays now in a neighborhood of the city to sing.

To learn songs for daily life. To lean sacred songs that correspond to our lineage. Songs to venerate the power of the land, its newness.

We'll continue to recover our memory.

fill Mapu kiñekisungey ka inchiñ ka tüfa püllungey,
all of the land is one soul and we're part of it.

fachi züngun

kizu ta neyümekey kiñe makawa
ñi püllüftrülke mew pelmu ta üremkülelu ngati
ñichi ñüzüftrülke ñi trülkepüle tuwlu
fey trongküpulu pu keltewe ñi kümkapüle llenga
itro alümapu

kiñeke mew
rakizuamtufiüm ta wenumapu
kiñe mañkengeketun ütrüftükuwlu trafyé wütre mu
wirüfnenturpulu ñi müpü pu pewen ñi yungum mew

pu zeyiñ kay kewlunuwi changüllkuwü mew
fey tralkanelelenew pu awükaye awka
pilkomollfüñ mew

ka fachi züngun
mellfümu mülechi trufken llengati
küpa traytraykowtuy lipüng mu

tuwün püle
tuway ñi ütrünarün tañi ngüman
wirarün
ñüküf ñi zumiñwelling püle puwlewüla ngati

esta voz

ella respira en la membrana
de un tambor remojado en la garganta
desde la piel de cueros costurados
hasta la aguada de los teros
lejos

a veces
cuando pienso las alturas
soy un cóndor que se arroja contra el frío
arrancándose las alas en el filo de los pinos

y los volcanes se hacen llamas en los dedos
y me truenan los potros torturados en las venas

y esta voz
que es cenizas en los labios
pretende ser cascada en el desierto

desde la sangre caer mi llanto
gritar
hasta el abismo del silencio

this voice

she breathes the membrane
of a drum soaked in a throat
stretching from a skin of stitched leather
to the distant
watery lapwing

sometimes
when i think of heights
i'm a condor throwing herself against the cold
thrashing her wings over a sharp crest of pine

and volcanos become flames in my fingers
and tortured foals thunder in my veins

and this voice
that's ash on the lips
wants to be a waterfall in the desert

my sobs surging from my blood
shouting
into an abyss of silence

zomokepüñeñ

I

iñche miauwfun
witruzomo reke mongen mew
kuñiltukechi peiküñn
chem pileyengün iñche mew
fentren meshazomo fütalafken mew

Ka llegüñmangen
epu püñeñ liwenpüñeñ
fentren nge nieyngu
wilüf ñi choñiwn

Amuyngu ñi ngülümam
ñi küme elkünuam pu antü
lichi, trivisol ka vitina mew
ramtulaingu kontuenew

II

llegüñeingu
puchallwa llüfkeingun zumiñ mew
mülefuyngün pu ngiñngo
meli witran mapu mo

Kimüyu tufa chi llükan
nielayu kofke ka wentelteku takun
eymu mew

hijas

I

yo andaba
tan derramada por la vida
dando lástima imagino
qué dirían de mí
tan regalada al mar

y me nacieron
dos hijas madrugadas
de innumerables ojos
brillantes impacientes

vinieron a juntarme
me ordenaron los días
en estantes de leche
trivisol
y vitina

sin consultar siquiera
me invadieron

II

nacieron
y los peces relampaguearon en la oscuridad
y hubo fauces por los cuatro costados

aprendimos el lacerante miedo
de no tener pan
y abrigo
para ustedes

daughters

I

i walked
through life so defeated
i'd pitifully imagine
them saying of me
so lost at sea

then two dawn daughters
were born to me
with brilliant restless
innumerable eyes

they came to repair me
organized my days
in shelves of milk
enfamil
and vitina

without even asking
they'd invaded me

II

they were born
and fish flashed in the darkness
and there were jaws in the four corners

we learned the biting fear
of having no bread
or shelter
for them

III

müna newen
epu pichiche newenkülelu
lloftuingu kiñe trow
ñi chaytuam fey engu ñi pelo
fentren pelo
ñi awka rüf zungu

Iñchiu mew itro
newenkünuwuyu
ka fey engu fütrangeyngu

IV

Tunten mew zewma pepilan
tufachi küruf ütruftuenew wirko trufken
ka nieenew tüfeymew iñche chongün

Wirarüngün ka nülayngu tufachi fanepuerta
rupayngu ñi ayen mew wente pilutüngkülen
küpalüyngu kiñe chozrayen
kümenümün niey pünantükuy tufachi baldío mew
iñche mew

iñche mulen
femngechi
nepelen kura reke

iney piay
mulean tüfa mew
fillke rupa winole engu

III

qué resistencia de personitas
al acecho
de un resquicio una fisura
por donde filtrar su luz
su desbandada luz
su verdad insoportable

justo a nosotros
que nos hacemos los fuertes
justo a nosotros
que nos quedan grandes

IV

y cuando ya no puedo?
cuando el viento me arroja paladas de ceniza
y ya casi me tiene
ahí
apagada

abren a gritos la puerta más pesada
pasan a risas sobre el silencio más sordo
y me traen ¿para mí?
una flor amarilla de esas
que pegotean su perfume en el baldío

se van
tras el amigo nuevo que junta cascarudos

yo me quedo así
recordada
como una piedra

quién lo diría
voy a estar aquí
cada vez
que vuelvan

III

what resistance by such little people
lying in wait
in a crack a fissure
through which filters their light
their disordering light
their unbearable truth

just for us
making us stronger
just for us
who feel dwarfed by them

IV

and when i can't go on?
when the wind slaps me with blows of ash
and pins me
there
near extinguished

they shout open the heaviest door
break out in laughter over the most deafening silence
and bring   for me?
one of those yellow flowers
wet with perfume from wild land

they go
following a new friend who collects horn beetles

that way i stay
remembered
like a stone

who says
i will be here
every time
you return

pu zomo engu mawün

fey chi pichikezomongeiñ amuiñ
montulngeiñ lepün mew
antü inantükueiñ mew kawellutu
welu küyen elürpaeiñ mew ñi pu ko nepeiñ mew
tüfey pun peiñ kiñe lom metawe, llawe pelaiñ

pu machikimelpeyel
llegiñ, feley, mülum mew
pepikawküleiñ, pu wampu ñi leliael ñamkülelu
ngenoshumelkezomo chiway mew
mawünwünn mew tapülfüna iñ kug
witrañpramlu wenu mew

keipüleimew ayün püñeñaimi
trapelngelaimi, llowaimi,
nge treifunakümlu mew, ñuin ayen ñi llallitun
mülekayay chi fainu eimi mi putramew
llükaalu am ñukengealu
kom kizulenche ñi ñuke miawlu rupu mew

wau mangitripalu chafozüaeimew
pu ishim zungulalu mew
traigen mew chem pepi pilaymi
welu llowaimi ñi wütruael pichi ñochi
chaliaimi, piaimi nien mawün
alütripaimi alüpramülewe mew
lafken mew wenu mew
ka ngütrawtuay lafkenkachu pu lom mew

las mujeres y la lluvia

cuando niñas vamos sueltas por el patio
y el sol nos persigue de a caballo
pero la luna implacable nos va dejando sus mareas
hasta que nos desvela
y esa noche encontramos
un cántaro
en lugar de la cintura

aprendices de machi las mujeres
nacemos así al rocío
listas para mirar los barcos que se pierden
descalzas a la neblina antes de que amanezca
nervaduras de lluvia nuestras manos
levantadas al cielo

te salpicará el amor
parirás sin amarras
y recibirás con ojos arrasados
la visita intermitente de la risa
permanecerá la llovizna en tu vientre
porque no te atreverás a ser la madre
de todos los desamparos
que andan por la calle

caudal desubicado te desarmará
en pájaros que no saben hablar
a borbotones no podrás decir
lo que quisieras
mejor dejarlo que se derrame despacio
decir
permiso tengo lluvia y alejarse
a una altura al mar al cielo
hasta que vuelvan a apretarse los musgos
en las profundidades

women and the rain

as girls we're loosed through the patio
and the sun gallops after us
till the implacable moon hits us with her tides
and we go sleepless
and that very night find
a jug
in place of a waist

machi apprentices we women
are born like this to dew
poised to watch over boats that lose their way
barefoot in the mist before daybreak
our hands ribbings of rain
raised to the sky

love will splash you
you'll give birth unmoored
and receive with wet eyes
intermittent visits of laughter
a drizzle persisting in your belly
because you'd never dare to be mother
to all the abandoned
walking the street

you'll be disarmed by the odd flood
of birds that can't speak
in flowing terms and you'll be unable to say
what you want
so better to let it spill out slowly
to say
forgive me i have rain and then depart
to the heights of the sea the sky
till the moss tightens again
in the depths

iñche kimün pu zomo turpu kamapukünuwlay

nülafingun chi wülngiñ ñi pu chirif
ka ngümaingün
ülpuingun chi fochon ekull
kütrüfingun, kafliftuyngün, katrüyngun pu cebolla
ngütantuyngün, lepüyngun, runkayngun pichikeche mew
küchayngun
chew kimüyngun

ka zomo rulpayngun ñi mongen
ñomümishimüyngun
ayülayngun ñi weyun ñi eluzungunon
pütokoy chi kaiñe
elkayngun ñi mülenon ñi mollfun amulewelalu anümche mew
pu zomo külliyngün ailiñ nütram mew, likan nütram mew
katakonuyngun rangiñ kaiñe

iñche nütramrakizuamün
nütramwitranentun perkan mew
pepi montulün aimeñ nütamtakuñman
atahualpa ñi mamüll üikülelu
tüfa nütram eluafiñ tüfeichi zomo
wütrungentulu, tüfeichi zomo katrütufingun ñi pu ishim

kiñechi   febrero mew, iñche mülen tüfey mew mapu mew
kom mawün müley
kiñeazngefuy kai kai ñi illku wente iñchiñ
wutrengey ko
pu kushe petulüyngün chi ngillatun
mülen ñi femagel

chumül müten yeiñ
trañmaleufü katrütufinge rume mawün
mapu ptokolay mapu rulmelay
chem no rume ngelaiñ

yo conozco mujeres que nunca se alejan

le abren la compuerta a sus gorriones
y lloran
enjuagan el trapo mojado lo estrujan
limpian con él la tabla
pican cebollas
igual hacen las camas
barren la casa peinan a los chicos
igual lavan
dónde aprendieron

hay otras que se pasan la vida domesticando
a sus pájaros
porque no quieren que irrumpan sin aviso
y los beba el enemigo
guardan su sangre su ausencia quietos en el fondo
y apuntan con palabras nítidas de cuarzo
que van a dar al blanco

yo a las palabras las pienso
y las rescato del moho que me enturbia
cada vez puedo salvar menos
y las protejo
son la leña prendida de atahualpa
que quisiera entregar a esas mujeres
las derramadas las que atajan sus pájaros

una vez en febrero yo estaba ahí
en el campo
y se llovía todo
parecía la furia de kay kay sobre nosotros
el agua estaba helada
las ancianas prosiguieron el ritual
y tuve que quedarme

i know women who never leave

who open the gate to their sparrows
and weep
who rinse a wet rag wring it out
clean the counter with it
dice onions
and just the same make every bed
sweep the house comb their kids' hair
wash right there
where they learned

still others go through life domesticating
their birds
so they don't barge in without notice
and fall to the enemy
women who motionlessly guard their blood their absence down deep
and take aim in clear words of quartz
that hit their mark

i think of words
and save them from the mildew that muddies me
though each time i can save fewer
but i protect them
they're atahualpa's lit firewood
that he wanted to give these women
the spilt those who curb their birds

one february i was there
in the field
and it poured down
on us like kay-kay's rage
the water was icy
the matriarchs kept on with the ritual
and i had to stay there

tiza wiri ñamümlu ko mew

pu pataka tripantü mew
chi antü nülakünuy pu tromu
meridiana epulef ñi füchazüngun
witrañpramuy kawellu taüll
rakizuamün kallfuwenu pepingeafuy
tüfa relmu kallfuwenu pepingeafuy
pu kawellu witrünkülelu
moro zaino pangare tostado bayo
chalifingun afmapu

küme nümüi mapu rupan füchamawün

hasta cuándo aguantaremos
pará la lluvia dios es demasiada
no la bebe la tierra se atraganta
y somos casi nada
trazos de tiza borrados por el agua

después de unos siglos el sol abrió las nubes
a voz gastada de meridiana epulef
levantó el taill del cauelo
pensé que dios podía ser ese arco iris
o los caballos en fila
moro zaino pangaré tostado bayo
saludando al horizonte despejado

huele tan bien la tierra después del aguacero

as long as we could endure
dear god stop the rain it's too much
the land can't drink it chokes
and we're almost nothing
chalk-tracings erased by the flood

a few centuries later the sun split the clouds
the tired voice of the split meridian
raised the sacred song of trees

and i thought god could be the rainbow
or the row of horses
black brown tan pony
saluting the cloudless sky

the earth smells so good after a downpour

pu zomo engu kürüf

fey wiñolekey
pepikawenew chi griega
rulpalu chi kafe bora
pifuenew kiñe wentru mew
inche rakizuamfun ta chi kürüf mew

chi kürüf wiñokey
welu tüfa waria wimlay
miawi
fillke rupa
auka rüpüwaria mew
kuyümkoron mew
ñamüntrekaneiñ mew

chi pu ishüm
üpünüingün
chi pu nümün pu takun pinüfüingün
pepikawlay chi ruka
chi kim chillfuy
feymew
müley iñ tükuael chi pava
pepikaael kiñeke mate
üngümael ñi amun
kiñekeantü mew
regleantü
¡iñey kimi!
kuyentrafkintu mew

reke kiñe llükafalkürüf
ngerkefuy chi malon
kiñe meulen traf chi pu antü
yafüngellele rume chi kuificheyem
reke pulil

las mujeres y el viento

él siempre va a volver
me previno la griega
traduciendo la borra del café
y me hablaba de un hombre
yo pensaba en el viento

el viento siempre vuelve
pero esta ciudad no se acostumbra
anda
cada vez
desaforado por las calles
a brochazos de tierra
borrándonos los pasos

se nos vuelan los pájaros
los olores
la ropa
se desafina la casa
la memoria se astilla
y hay que poner la pava
preparar unos mates
y esperar
a que se vaya
en unos días
unas semanas
vaya a saber
con el cambio de luna

como un tremendo viento
dicen que fue el malón
un torbellino en contra de los días
y eso que los antiguos eran duros
como rocas
firmes

women and the wind

he'll always return
the greek warned me
translating the coffee grounds
and she spoke to me of a man
i thought of wind

the wind always returns
though this city is never ready
it goes
each time
whipping through the streets
erasing our footsteps
with great brushstrokes of earth

birds
colors
clothes all fly from us
the house goes off kilter
memory splinters
it's time to heat the kettle
prepare mate
and wait
until it's gone
in a few days
a few weeks
we'll know
by the change of moon

they say indian raids
were like a fierce wind
a tornado against the days
and the ancients were hard
as rocks
firm

newenküley rume
tüfeymew mülen ñi mollfüñ

püdüm
pifuen chuchu
ni kimngey chi laufken
iñche wefn ofülül kiñe ünu

faw chi pun rupa pürnagi
chi kürüf raraüi
kacharnentulu chi pu apill rupa
mülekaiñ
chi pu wingkul chafküleyngün
tüfeymew maiwi ignacia quintulaf ñi ngillatun
wiñolalu am ñi piñeñ
yerwefitruñ
azukarfitruñ
pralu
zoy taüll
ürkütunantüngey ñi züngun

chi kürüf wiñokeley
küpa yerpueiñ küpa malüy iñ pu follil
yeniey kiñeke zomo wingüdnentueyew engün
wallkiaweyew engün
iñche zoy ayün tüfey fanelay ke rütron
tüfa trongekeforo mew
pafialu traf cemento

fey wiñolekey
welu llükanienge
yom fey pifuy
chi griega
amualuam fey

chi kürüf llochoy
chi nagmapu ailinkünuwi

ahí quedó su sangre
desparramada
me decías abuela
y tu recuerdo es el lago
al que me asomo
para sorber un trago

y aquí hasta la noche se ha opacado
el viento ruge
arrancando hasta las ganas de quedarse
seguro que las lomas quedaron peladitas
por ahí andará el ruego de ignacia quintulaf
porque su hijo no volvía
el humo de la yerba y el azúcar quemadas
subiendo apenas
un poco más que el taill
y es una pausa su voz

el viento siempre vuelve
quiere rendirnos a nosotras
probarnos las raíces
llevarse algunas
arrastradas
o girando
yo prefiero esas matas livianas
a estos huesos espesos
que reventarán contra el cemento

él siempre va a volver
pero no tenga miedo
agregaba
la griega
porque también se irá

el viento amaina
y el planeta se pone transparente

there lay their blood
spilt
you'd tell me grandma
and your memory is the lake
i look upon
to savor a drink

and here the dark of night has fallen the wind roars
shredding any desire to stay
certain the hills were stripped
perhaps ignacia quibtulaf's plea will go out
because her son never returned
steam off mate and burnt sugar
barely wafting up
over the sacred song
and her voice is a pause

the wind always returns
wants to defeat us
test our roots
carry some away
dragged off
or sent spinning
i prefer those light plants
to these heavy bones
that crash against cement

he'll always return
but don't fret
added
the greek
because he'll also leave again

the wind dies down
and the planet comes clear

kiñe olmo ta tüfa
ñi lamngen zichoy
kiñe foron kiñeketapül
ñümilu kintulu
rakizuamn ñi küpaliael
ñi fün boulevard mew chi kürüf
¿peymi? faw müley ka

iñche küpa pin
ricardo
ñi pu yall pelongeyngün
reke tüfa engün olmo
welu petu nien kuyüm
chi pu troi mew
ka mülelayngün züngun

iñey kimi chew nganküleeyew engün
chi kürüf

éste es un olmo
y señala mi hermano
un tallo y unas hojas
alzándose del suelo
desafiantes
pienso que el viento nos trajo su semilla
desde el boulevard
y ¿ves? aquí hay otro

quiero decir
ricardo
tus hijos son tan claros
como estos olmos
pero tengo todavía
arena
en las coyunturas
y no hay palabras

quién sabe adónde
las estará sembrando
el viento

this is an elm
says my brother signaling
a stem and a few leaves
rising from ground
defiant
i believe the wind brought its seed
from the boulevard
and look, here's another

i want to say
ricardo
your children are clear
as these elms
but i still have
sand
in my joints
and i have no words

who knows where
the wind sews
its seed

pu zomo engu wütre

iñche kimun wütre feichi pichizomongen
guardapolvo mew
dumiñkuley
iñche ñi chaw ñi rambler clasic amulafuy
müley iñ namuntuael eskuela mew
katrütuantüiñ
chi pu wafün foro kataeyew iñ pichi ilo
iñchengefun kiñekeluku kutrafulu
pifuiñ müna wütre
ta iñ leliael chi puzüngu ñi kuyuan
iñ kompañküleael

chi pu ñuke kom
wütreleyngun
iñche ñi ñuke pichizomongey
cushamen mew miawi alpargata mew piren mew
kintumapulu pu kapura
iñche konümpanien ñi ñuke
ñi chokonkenamun
ka kiñe weshazuam kapura
tufey engün pofo ñamlu
ka müley ñi kintuchenorume

ñi ñuke eñumngeeiñ mew
feyngey kiñe konkülen
müley ñi eñumngeael pichikeche
ruku furi namun pilun
feypi ka tremingün ñi pu changkiñ ñi pu tapül
newenmaeyew engün pichikeche pukem mew
ka kiñeke mew tripapayantü ka feyengün
takuleingün
tremtremyelu am pu lipang
müley iñ wellimael tüfey pichikechangkiñ
ñochizüngun mew

las mujeres y el frío

yo al frío lo aprendí de niña en guardapolvo estaba
oscuro
el rambler clasic de mi viejo no arrancaba
había que irse caminando hasta la escuela
cruzábamos el tiempo
los colmillos atravesándonos
la poca carne
yo era unas rodillas que dolían
decíamos qué frío
para mirar el vapor de las palabras
y estar acompañados

las mamás todas
han pasado frío
mi mamá fue una niña que en cushamen
andaba en alpargatas por la nieve
campeando chivas
yo nací con la memoria de sus pies entumecidos
y un mal concepto de las chivas
esas tontas que se van y se pierden
y encima hay que salir a buscarlas
a la nada

mi mamá nos abrigaba
ella es como un adentro
hay que abrigar a los hijos
el pecho   la espalda   los pies y las orejas
dicen así
y les crecen las ramas y las hojas
y defienden a los chicos del invierno
y a veces sale el sol y ellas tapando
porque los brazos se les van en vicio
y hay que sacarles despacio
con palabras esos gajos

women and the cold

as a girl in overalls i learned the cold
was dark
when my father's rambler classic wouldn't start
meaning we'd walk to school
cutting through weather
fangs biting into
our scant flesh
i was two knees that ached
we'd say what cold
to see the vapor of our breath
and have company

all mothers
have endured the cold
my mother was a girl in cushamen
wore slippers in the snow
pasturing goats
i was born with the memory of her frozen feet
and a bad impression of goats
those dopes that wander and get lost
so you have to set out to find them
in all that vastness

my mother used to bundle us up
she who is like an interiority
children must be bundled up
chest   back   feet and ears
they say it like that
and they grow the branches and leaves
and defend the children against winter
and even when the sun comes out they're still bundling
because their arms move by habit
and those layers must be removed slowly
with words

welu chi wütre rumel ngelay
iñche kim
tüfey pun epulef lof mew
umerküleiñ wallrupa mew iñ piwke lifmapu mew
eufemia ürkütufuy kamarikunpurun mew
ka chi pun reyimi ñi pichikal chi kachu mew

wünngefuy
eufemia nepey
chi trangliñ chi kal mew
ka chi wütre tüfey rupa wünniefuy
ka newenayefuy engu inchiñ
füchaley tüfa wütre
pieiñ mew

chi pu zomo kimuiñ alüantü
iñ nieael kiñe antü mongen mew
amulelu chillkalelu kiñe kutral rüpü
waria mew
welu zuamnielaiñ
kimlan chem mew llamngkum tüfachi
tüfey rupanantu iñche zuamngefun
pu karukal media
rüpüwaria katrütulu

chi pu waria mew
wütre yifküeiñ mew chi pu lüli
katay fozkapel mew
yom trürngey
femnechi miawfun
ka chi pun mew
mulefuy kiñe wentru iñche ñi kawitu
ka kiñe pichiwechengey ka kiñe konangey
iñche küpa neyülafun newen mew

pero el frío no siempre
lo sé porque esa noche en aldea epulef dormíamos
apenas
alrededor de nuestro corazón al descampado.
eufemia descansaba el purrún del camaruco
y la noche confundió su pelo corto con el pasto

era la madrugada y eufemia despertó
con la helada en el pelo
y el frío esa vez tenía boca
y se reía con nosotras
se está poniendo viejo el frío nos decían

las mujeres aprendemos tarde
que hay un tiempo en la vida
en que hasta sin intención
vamos dejando una huella de incendio
por el barrio
ni sé por qué la perdemos
y esa tarde yo precisaba
medias de lana cruda para cruzar las calles

en las ciudades el frío
nos raspa las escamas
punza en la nuca
se vuelve más prolijo
en eso andaba y a la noche
había un hombre en mi cama
o era un niño o un muchacho
yo no quería respirar muy fuerte

but i don't always know
the cold because that night in aldea epulef
we barely slept
in the barren field around our heart.
eufemia slept the dance of camaruco
and the night confused your short hair with the grass

it was dawn and eufemia woke
with ice in her hair
and this time the cold had a mouth
and it laughed with us
telling us the cold is getting old

we women learn late
that there's a time in life
when we unintentionally
leave burning footprints
throughout the neighborhood
i don't know how we miss it
and this afternoon i need
wool socks to traverse the streets

in cities the cold
rakes our flesh
pricks our nape
grows verbose
i was in it and at night
there would be a man in my bed
or a child or boy
i didn't want to breathe deeply

niey kümeketakuwkug
tüfa wentru
fey mew chem mew iñche amun
pelu ñi kintuael iñche
ñi aftükuenew
kulafawlul pu ishümreforo
iñche ñi ange mew

chumngechi ükümaukün ngean
pelalu am iñche

tremokünuwlu

yom müley
uyülen
tüfa wütre mew
kallfümollfüñ wütre

tiene las manos abrigadas este hombre
entonces por qué me fui
para ver si salía a buscarme o me dejaba a que los
esqueletos de pájaros
se incrusten en mi cara

como el eco del silencio seré
si no me encuentra

por hacerme la linda

encima me da abismo
este frío
sangre azul

the man had bundled hands
so why did i leave
to see if he'd set out to find me or leave me
so that skeletons of birds
could embed themselves in my face

i will be like the echo of silence
if i'm not found

to make myself pretty

this cold
blue blood
that opens in me an abyss

ngellípun üngümafiel ti colectivo

üngüm colectivolechi pu
ütrüfkünuye ñi señor
chongümelkünukilnge fachi püchü lewlew
ré antümu ingkánengel llengá wenté tranglíñ

matú küpápe ti colectivo
ta üngümün lle
wirkólkey trufkén tólmew ngatí
fey mülí tañi kupáfneafielmaye maychüleal
ka lüyükünumekeal chi rüpü mew
epúrume zuámfule wüme ti pu pilkómollfüñ
wüñówitrawnewün

ütrüfkünuye ñi señor
felén rupákinolpe
topákenolu reké ta iñché tañi tritráng namúnküyawal
ayüwmakenolu reké ta iñché tañi kümé piwkéngeal kiñe
ronóngelu reké
kiñe üngkó iñínorume chémnorume

meñólen küpákinolpe señor
kizú ñi züngú mütén inánekelleyngün ngatí
feymay namúnmayew rültrékawün
ka kiñe wifká langümüymanew ñi ayén
fey tutéwnarün trüylítuwe pülé yeniéngechi kullíñ

alüñmakinolpe señor fachántü ta wütrengí
fey may chi pu pewmá nga ám mew ta puwláy ka fachi
itró küñüwun mew ngeñíñmakünukeli püchüñma
élkünufili chi rüngán
fey pepí kafküngüchatukünufili
chi epéwün

oración para esperar el colectivo

señor de los desamparados
que esperan el colectivo
no permitas que se apague esta llamita
defendida a puro sol sobre la escarcha

que el colectivo venga pronto
pues la espera
amontona cenizas en la frente
y tengo que apalearlas y hacer señas
y asomar los ojos a la ruta
aunque las venas duden
tironeando

señor de los desamparados
que no pase de largo
como si yo no fuera capaz de andar descalza
como si yo no fuera propensa a la ternura
como si fuera una chapa
un poste   nadie   nada

y que no venga lleno señor
porque se salen con la suya
entonces patas y empujones
en un boleto me suicidan la sonrisa
y me resigno animal al matadero

que no demore señor hoy hace frío
y no llegan los sueños hasta el alma
en el filo de este riesgo no me culpes
si abandono un segundo la trinchera
y alcanzo a maldecir
la madrugada

prayer while waiting for the bus

father of the helpless
waiting for the bus
don't let die this tiny flame
fueled by pure sun amidst frost

may the bus come soon
while the wait
piles ash upon my brow
and i work to brush it off and signal
and keep my eyes on the route
even if my veins doubt it
tugging

father of the helpless
don't let it pass
as if i weren't capable of walking barefoot
as if i weren't prone to tenderness
as if i were a bottle cap
a post   no one   nothing

and father may it not arrive full
because they'll rob you blind
the stomps and shoves
with a ticket they kill my smile
and i settle in a beast headed to butcher

may it not be delayed   father   today it's cold
and dreams can't reach the soul
on the brink of such risk   don't blame me
if i abandon the trench for a second
and manage to curse
the dawn

ti ramtun

fentekünun, kiñe ramtun inche reke
müchampramyu iñ namun
miawleaiñ
kiñe nüyün ñi trawau ti furi mew
nielay pu newen folil
fürenelay

wimn ñi kimnon
layaiñ kiñe epew mew ka epew
mangitripaiñ, pangküiñ ti pu ramtun
trawa ñi pu kaño mew
pu foro püle

miawiyaiñ
pu che inchiñ reke
pu kewan sechukünuleiñ
newenküleiñ pu pewma ñi mollfüñkug

leliwüaiñ teifunruka
ti mapa ñi pewma mew

pregunta

habrá que resignarse a ser pregunta
arremangarse los pies
seguir andando
con un golpe de sismo por espalda
sin cimientos
ni contemplaciones

habrá que acostumbrarse sin respuesta
morir en una historia y otra historia
salir de madre pateando las preguntas
por los caños de la piel
hasta los huesos

y andar
humano no más
apuntalando luchas
controlando el pulso de la tierra

mirarse escombro en
el mapa de los sueños

question

she'll have to resign herself to being a question
roll her pants up
keep walking
with a seismic blast in her back
with neither foundation
nor contemplation

she'll have to get used to no answer
to dying in story after story
to being born kicking questions
from the shell of her skin
to her bones

and to go on
human no more
enduring fights
controling the earth's pulse

seeing herself as ruins
on the map of dreams

dios nüfi kiñe antü

dios nüfi kiñe antü
tufa chi fill mapu ñi antü
kütrüfi
kiñe papel reke

tufachi antü
wirüftuantü
chizküy
fine, funanko,
colüarkenko

wüni
tripaiñ tapül mew
tronopüllü engu

piwiñ antüare mew
pepilngelayngun pu rayen

dios agarra un día

dios agarra un día
de este mundo
y lo estruja
como si fuera un papel

el día desflorado
destila semen
agua de cloaca
y marea roja

después amanece
salimos de la hoja
con el alma arrugada
y nos secamos al sol

como flores imposibles

god grabs a day

god grabs a day
from this world
and crumples it
like paper

a deflowered day
drips semen
cloaca water
and red tide

then dawn breaks
we leave the leaf
with a wrinkled soul
and dry ourselves in the sun

like impossible flowers

kiñe wentru

üwemapu ñi rangiantü

pu kura dulli kiñe wentru

kura wentepramuy kura
ültrey wekuñ püle

ürkütuy
rekülkünuwi ti wentru ñi furi
tufachi kuzaw zeumalayay
chumnkaonorume

dios fülfi ti wentru ñi tol
ti wenu mew

un hombre

el sol al mediodía del desierto

un hombre elige piedras

piedra encastra piedra
apunta al menhir

descansa
apoya la espalda
sobre su obra nunca concluida

dios le toca la frente con el cielo

man

midday desert sun

a man is choosing stones

lays stone upon stone
to raise a menhir

he rests
leans his back
on his unfinished work

god touches the man's brow with sky

epu llafinge ñi furi mew

epu llafinge ñi furi mew
trepeleiñ
tufachi pewma mew
kiñe füu ñi pelo
llüfkey

upetun
trekawan ka pefiñ ñi pu llowzungun

kimniekan ñi pepi üpütun pewma mew
üpütun senchu
trafopüraprawe ka ñi alüpran ñüküfküley
fiñmangelukewentru

chem iñchengefun?
tunté fanelai iñche ñi namun
lefüfun senchu ti pun
mulefun anka wenu mew?
chem zungu yefun?
chem uyülonkon lanüeneu iñche ñi llikakenge?
chem ayetuchen ügürufi iñche ñi falke
ka aftükueneu
trepelen ka üpül mew?
kiñe che amulpungey trafkintu mew?
kiñe che azueyew
iñche ñi wicharümüpü üküm engu?

kimn
kimlafun ñi akun
winteyüy ñi likmüpün
fanelay, chiwai mew
kimn

detrás de los párpados

detrás de los párpados queda la vigilia detenida
en el sueño un haz de luz centellea
y sospecho
que un paso más acá están las respuestas

recuerdo que en sueños
puedo volar
y vuelo
sobre escaleras rotas alturas silenciosas
y hombres que espían

¿qué fui yo?
¿qué delicados pies tenía
que corría sobre el cuerpo de la nocheaire?
¿qué mensaje llevaba?
¿qué vértigo me hundió los ojosmiedo?
¿qué burla corrosiva tocó mi hombro
y me abandonó despierta en la otra orilla?
¿alguien fue enviada en mi lugar?
¿alguien curó mis alas rasgadas por el silencio?

sé
que no supe llegar a destino
y que se desarmó mi vuelo leve y blanco en la neblina
y que estoy condenada en cada sueño
a repetir el intento

behind my eyelids

behind my eyelids a detained world waits
in the dream a cord of light sparkles
and i think
the answers are but a step away

i recall how in dreams
i can fly
and i fly
over broken stairs   silent heights
and men who spy

what was i?
what delicate feet did i have
that ran across the body of nightair?
what message did i carry?
what dizziness undid my eyefear?
what caustic taunt touched my shoulder
and left me awake on the other shore?
was someone sent in my place?
did someone mend my wings slashed by silence?

i know
i didn't know how to reach the destination
and that my airy white flight came apart in the mist
and that i'm condemned with each dream
to repeat the attempt

wülngen zungu ñi pepipepiltun
feyentuan
pepian katarumefin llafinge
ñi müpün mew

ka wewawn
ti wünn ti mapu mew
epu allfen engu
iñche ñi furi mew

hasta que pueda
fervorosa
traspasar en vuelo los párpados de la vigilia
y me gane

amanecer al mundo
con dos cicatrices
en la espalda

until i fervent
in flight

can break through the eyelids' barrier and seize
a dawning world
with two scars on my back

iñche pekefiñ ti pichikeluan kechan kiyawlu

iñche pekefiñ ti pichikeluan kechan kiyawlu ale
kuyentulelu

feichi wefüngun
ti pukem chalintükuwi
takulu kal mew ka ñochirüna mew
Iñche pekefiñ ti neyen trüntrünülu
allushanka rangi mew
ñi kizungenewn ka ñi ñochiayun
wirafküleyengun engun
kizungechi mapu mew

iñche pekefiñ rakizuamün
yaf mañumtufalin
iñche pekefiñ ti pichikeluan ka mapu mew

iñche lliwan zoy petu miauwan
Iney kimy tunten
wewllukanlu püllepuan   feyengun mew
trokiwalu pichikeluan ñi pu nge mew, rume alükonn
nge engun
llownlu afmatulu piren ñi tünkülen mew
piren püntünentuy poz ka afpunketroltro

iñche tragtuli pepilngeay
pepi nüfüluwn lifkenge mew afpungenulunge mew
pepi ünkotun kiñe pichiantü
rangi antü mew

ñi kizungenewn ka ñi ñochiayuwn
wirafküleyengun engun
kizungechi kom mapu mew

yo he visto a los chulengos

yo he visto a los chulengos en manada
iluminados por la luna

cuando aparecen ellos
el invierno se entrega
cubierto de pelusas y de lana
he visto el aire estremecido entre sus ancas tibias
y a la libertad y a la ternura
galopando con ellos
sueltas
por la tierra

he visto   creo
más de lo que merezco:
he visto a los chulengos desde lejos

yo presiento que he de andar más todavía
quién sabe cuánto
hasta vencer el miedo de acercarme hasta ellos
para medirme en sus ojos tan profundos de espacio
y aceptar el milagro de un silencio de nieve
que desprenda la costra los últimos abrojos

si resisto es posible que me permitan ellos
sumergirme en sus ojos ingenuos infinitos
estaquearme un instante
en el centro del tiempo

ser la libertad ser la ternura
galopando con ellos
sueltos
por la tierra

i've seen the chulengos

i've seen a herd of chulengos
lit by the moon

when they appear
winter submits
covered in lint and wool
i've seen the air tremble in their warm haunches
and the freedom and the tenderness
galloping with them
loosed
upon the land

i've seen i think
more than i deserve
i've seen the chulengos from afar

i sense the need to push on
who knows how far
to conquer my fear of getting near them
to measure myself in the deep space of their eyes
and accept the miracle of a silence of snow
that removes the scab   the final thistle

if i can hold out they might allow me
to submerge myself in their eyes   infinite little ones
to stake myself for an instant
in the center of time

to be freedom to be tenderness
galloping with them
loosed
upon the land

feichi lali mulen ñi nontual katrutuleufun

feichi lali mülen ñi nontual katrütuleufün
chem trewa ngiyulaenew, nielan trewa
trongli trewa nümüalu ñi llükanten
amuay ina inche

kushe müleay nontuwe mew
eluafiñ epu llanka
ñi nontuaetew
ti pu kura folilentuel
ñi kütikun mew
ñi pütra mew
ifümüchikekura kutranpiwkelelu
wirarün pepi wirarünoel
feichi ñi pu nge yifüingu
ka inche koilatufun ñi mongen

elutukuafiñ tüfa
yom nielaay chem no rume
mupiñ kechi pu külleñu
pepi pelafilu ñi llumümel ta ti mongen
amulu
pu alwe ñi furi mew
kintualu pu düwen
pu lalün
pu metawe
pu tapül

falilulüay kushe?

prayu ñi trewa iñchiu
nontuwe pinguzay rupanantü
ngulu mew

cuando me muera deberé cruzar el río

cuando me muera deberé cruzar el río
qué perro hará de guía si no tengo
un perro flaco que olerá mi cobardía
irá a mi lado

y estará la vieja en la balsa
le entregaré dos llankas
para que me cruce
las piedras arrancadas de cuajo
de mi garganta
de mi estómago
crecidas en los dolores
en los gritos que no pude gritar
cuando se agrandaban mis ojos
y hacía que vivía

entregaré esas piedras
y no habrá más
seguro lágrimas
porque no pude encontrarle el secreto a esta vida
porque me fui
detrás de los fantasmas
buscando tramas
y arañas
y cántaros
y hojas

¿reconocerá la vieja su valor?

subiremos con mi perro
la balsa se deslizará en la tarde
hacia el oeste

when i die i should cross the river

when i die i should cross the river
but what dog will guide me as i have none?
a skinny dog that smells my cowardice
will walk at my side

and the old lady will be in the boat
i'll give her two blue stones
to take me across
stones uprooted
from my throat
my stomach
cultivated in pain
in the shouts i couldn't hurl
when my eyes went wide
and made me alive

i'll hand over those stones
and nothing more
but tears
because i failed to find life's secret
because i went
after ghosts
chasing stories
and spiders
and jugs
and leaves

will the old lady know their worth?

my dog and i will climb aboard
the raft will slide into the afternoon
heading west

fentepuyu
müley ñi müleael ñi pichilamngen tie mew
müley ñi müleael
ti lan pepi ngelay kiñe chem no rume ti kiñeishim
iney wiri kütral

fey nieay pu pefalañken pu nge mew
yom pu refnge
kintuayngu inche mew
entuenew pu wayun
kolotuwüenew ti pu changüll mew
kiñe choikepünon

üiay kütral wente kallfükekura
winüngkü piwketuyu
mollfün mew inche ñi lamngen wiriay
kiñe kultrun ankawenu

feymew kimlayan
kiñe kawellungeli
ka kiñe neyüngeli
kurufngele kiñe trutruka

tripaayu wirafülu
püdümlu leufü ñi puwangelen
ka awün mew
kimuan kiñetu
chem ngey ngelu kiñe kona leflu kisungen lan mew
chem perimontu iüfueyew

wiñoyu mallin mew
kütral mew niey ti che
pu kuyulchalla ka küyen
pu alamo ñi filltapül wilüfülu

arribaremos
y tiene que estar allí mi hermana menor
tiene que estar
no puede ser la muerte una nada para un pájaro
para quien ha pintado con pinceles el fuego
ella tendrá cicatrices visibles en los ojos
sus ojos más certeros aún
hurgarán en mí
hasta sacarme las espinas
me dibujará el rostro con sus dedos
una huella de choique
arderá el fuego sobre piedras azules
comeremos corazones palpitantes
y mi hermana pintará un kultrun en el aire
con la sangre

después no sabré
si soy un caballo
o un resuello
si es el viento una trutuka
y saldremos galopando
a desparramar las estrellas del río
y en el movimiento circular
sabré de una vez
qué es ser un guerrero que corre libre hacia la muerte
qué visiones lo ardían

regresaremos al mallín
y habrá la gente alrededor del fuego
las ollas tiznadas y la luna
y cada hoja de los álamos brillando

we'll arrive
and my little sister has to be there
she has to be
death can't be a nothingness of fire
painted by paintbrush for a bird
she'll have visible scars in her eyes
eyes more focused than ever
that'll delve into me
pull every thorn from me
trace my face with her fingers
a rhea's footprint
the fire burning over blue stones
we'll eat beating hearts
and my sister will paint a kultrun in the air
with the blood

afterward i won't know
if i'm a horse
or a gasp
if the wind is a trutruka
and we'll go galloping
to cut loose the stars from the river
and in the circular movement
i'll know at once
what it is to be a warrior running freely towards death
what visions burn in him

we'll return to the green plain
and folks will be gathered around a fire
blackened pots and the moon
and every leaf on the poplar shining

feymew konümpafiñ
fentren kamapu
latuan

pu barrio rukawe
tremlu uyülonkon mew
waria afpun mapu mew
pu nylonwallka ka pu wangelen tie mew
pu cable kompuchepelomtuwe

entonces me recordaré
de ellos tan lejos
y moriré de nuevo

de los barrios planes de vivienda
creciendo en vértigo
en la ciudad con horizonte
las bolsas de nylon y las estrellas allí
entre los cables del alumbrado público.

so i'll remember
them from afar
and die once more

of the flat neighborhoods of home
rising in vertigo
from the city's horizon
plastic bags and the stars there
between the cables of the <u>illuminated public</u>.
                    street lights

kiñe azentu futa wariarupu 40 mo

senguer leufü püle ka Genoa pule
alünmaiñ iñ akun
fentre mate ka fentre ngutram
kuchalleliñ rume

rupaliñ futa wariarupu mo
pu lamngen
kiñe rupa amufuiñ Kopawe ñi pu trufken püle ka rupa
plang kürüf kangeitueiñ mew
tufachi rupa wiñoiñ ti chiway nülakünuiñ

rumel kintuleiñ ti pukintuwe
ñamümlafilu pünon

memoria ñi pu napa
kangeltuy mapu mew
tufa mew pu dinosaurios kurüyiwiñ mo

tufa mew kütral ñi pu trufken
fey, choikenamun, üiyümefi
fey lantufi ñi chau
fey amutuy, kimeleiñ mew:
ti kizulen, petu ünümafiñ

tufa mew pu neyün Orkeke engu Kasimiro yu kawel
kiñe amukan mo
Manshana Mapu püle

tufa mew puche memorianokechi
pu che witrapramlayngun pu lipang
kalfuwenufuchá kalfuwenukushe

una foto en la ruta 40

desde el río senguerr al genoa
no se llega más
por más mate y conversación
que vayamos lavando

si habremos andado por esta ruta
pu lamngen
una vez nos dirigíamos a las cenizas marrones del Copawe
otra, nos desconoció el viento blanco
esta vez, volvimos abriendo la neblina

siempre esforzando la vista
para no perder la huella

las napas de la memoria
se distinguen en la tierra
acá los dinosaurios ennegrecidos en su propio aceite

acá las cenizas de los fuegos que encendió
él de las patas de choike,
él que tuvo que matar a su padre,
él que se fue, enseñándonos la soledad de esperarlo
aún

acá el resoplido de los caballos de Orkeke y Casimiro
en uno de sus viajes
al Manzana Mapu

y acá los sin memoria
los que no levantaban más los brazos a
kalfuwenufuchá kalfuwenukushe

a photo on route 40

it no longer runs
from the senguerr river to the genoa
no matter how much mate and talk
we pour over

when we've walked the route
pu lamngen
it one time led us to Copawe's brown ash
another time disoriented us with white wind
this time we returned splitting fog

always straining our sight
not to miss footprints

the groundwater of memory
surges from the land
here dinosaurs blackened in their own oil

here the ash of the fires that burned
he of the choike feet
he who killed his father
he who left, teaching us the loneliness in waiting for him
still

here the snort of Orkeke's and Casimiro's horses
on one of their trips
to the Mapuche Applelands

and here those without memory
those who no longer raise their arms to
kalfuwenufuchá kalfuwenukushe

tufa mew chi pu wentru yafükünuwn
zewman lashu ñi pu trülke mo
nüniefin ka rupa chupey toro mo
füchañma mo
tremo
koatun chum pu kona
muleyngun tralkan mo

pu tralkan allkutuyngun iñ che
nürüftükuwn
iñ lonko Inakayal
pu sótano mo yañ museo
ñi holokausto

ay chum amuy ti memoria ayün mew
wenupray trürngey ti mülum firkümfiüy pu palipali
pranüy inal yu leufü

katrütunieiñ mew alumna tufa fucha wariarupu mo

tripaiñ neyen mapu mo müchameiñ mew
runkaeiñ mew trürngey pu neneo
zeumiñ kiñe azentu tufa azentun
recuerdo molaiñ

acá los hombres curtidos
como para hacer lazos con sus tientos
y sujetar otra vez al chupey toro
al tremendo
al hermoso
bramando como los konas
que se quedaron en los truenos

los truenos que escuchaba nuestra gente
encerrada
y nuestro lonko Inakayal
en los sótanos de ese museo del horror
del holocaust

ay cómo se va la memoria a la querencia
asciende como el rocío que enfría los tobillos
sube hasta las orillas de estos ríos

y nos detiene un rato en esta ruta

salimos al aire que nos dobla
nos peina como a neneos
y sacamos una foto de esta imagen
para la que no necesitamos el recuerdo.

here the men weather-beaten
as if ready to make lassos of rawhide
and subject again the bull Chupey
to the brutal
beautiful
bellowing like that of the konas
trapped in thunder

the thunder that our enclosed
people
and our lonco Inakayal heard
in the basement of this museum of the horrors
of the holocaust

o how the memory goes to its affections
rises like the dew that chills the ankles
rises to the banks of these rivers

and stops us a moment on this route

we go out into air that bends us
that combs our hair as if it were scrub brush
and we take a photo of this image
for which we need no reminder.

el idioma silenciado

Sólo fue hace cien años, sin embargo para mi generación parece que hubiese sido en un tiempo mítico. El pueblo mapuche se movía con libertad en su territorio, la gente se comunicaba con las fuerzas de la mapu. Mapuzungun significa el idioma de la tierra. La tierra habla, todos sus seres tienen un lenguaje y todos los mapuches lo conocían.

El mapuzungun era la primera lengua y se enseñaba y aprendía en condiciones óptimas. A la sombra de los ancianos crecían los nuevos brotes, el verde perfecto que luego estaba delante de los rituales. Cerca del agua.

Las mujeres cantaban los tayüles que transmitían la fuerza, y el orgullo de ser quien se era no era un tema filosófico en cuestión.

Pero la muerte que desde 1492 venía cercando a los pueblos originarios de América cerró su círculo en el sur. La guerra del desierto, el malón winka, significó la derrota militar, la ocupación del territorio por parte del estado argentino. "Cuando se perdió el mundo" hace cien años.

El mapuzungun se volvió el idioma para expresar el dolor, el idioma del desgarro cuando el reparto de hombres, mujeres y niños como esclavos. Un susurro secreto en los campos de concentración. El idioma del consuelo entre los prisioneros de guerra. El idioma para pensar.

Fue el idioma del extenso camino del exilio, la distancia del destierro. La larga marcha de nuestros bisabuelos hacia las reservas. Ka Mapu.

A nuestros abuelos, les tocó ir a la escuela rural y hacerse bilingües a la fuerza. Aunque fue el proscripto de la escuela y los maestros enseñaron a los niños a avergonzarse del idioma que hablaban en su hogar, el mapuzungun siguió vigente. La lengua de la tierra estaba en el aire de la oralidad y "la castilla", en la escritura borroneada de los cuadernos.

Antropólogos-lingüistas, ka mollfunche, hicieron intentos de escribirlo, armaron diccionarios y gramáticas. Así como intentaron atrapar el territorio entre los alambrados, intentaron atrapar el sonido del mapuzungun en grafemas occidentales.

the silenced language

Although it was only one hundred years ago, it seems to my generation like some mythical age. The Mapuche could roam freely across their territory and communicated with the elements of the mapu. Mapuzungun means "language of the land." The land speaks. All its beings have language, and the Mapuche know it.

Mapuzungun was the first language, and it was taught and learned in optimal conditions. In the shade of elders, new saplings grew, a perfect green preceding the rituals, near the water.

The women would sing their tayüles, which transmitted power, and the pride of being who one is was not a philosophical question.

But the death that has crept towards the First Peoples of the Americas since 1492 left no stone unturned in the south. The war for the desert, the winka raids, signaled military defeat and the occupation of territory by the Argentine state. "The end of the world" took place one hundred years ago.

Mapuzungun became the language for expressing pain, the language of despondence during the divvying up of men, women, and children as slaves. The clandestine whisper in the concentration camps. The language of solace among prisoners of war. The language for thought.

It was the language of the long road of exile, the distance of banishment. Of the harsh march of our great-grandparents to reservations, ka mapu.

Our grandparents were sent to rural schools and made bilingual by force. But however banned by the schools, where teachers shamed children for their home language, Mapunzungun endured. The language of the land was in the air of orality; Spanish in the writing crossed-out in workbooks

Linguistic anthropologists, ka mollfunche, tried to write it. They created dictionaries and grammar. Just as they tried to trap the territory within barbed-wire fences, so, too, did they try to trap the sound of Mapunzungun within western graphemes.

Pero al interior de nuestro pueblo la política del avergonzamiento hizo estragos. El mapuzungun pasó a ser un estigma, la marca de inferioridad de quienes ingresaban forzadamente al sistema capitalista, como mano de obra barata.

Tal vez fue una decisión de los ancianos el dejar de enseñarlo. ¿Pudieron reunirse? ¿Pudieron conversar en mapuzungun sobre el futuro? O simplemente callaron. Evaluaron que sus conocimientos ya no servirían, que los nuevos brotes podrían manejarse mejor sin ellos, en este nuevo mundo, siempre amenazante, siempre señalando, siempre acusando, siempre sonriendo.

El mapuzungun fue el idioma de la conversación de los ancianos, el idioma para convocar a las fuerzas en la intimidad del amanecer. El idioma para guardar. Para callar. La ciudad fue una posibilidad laboral y una posibilidad de estudio para los brotes. Se vinieron nuestros padres monolingües, sin ngillatun, sin mapuzungun. A cambiar el ciclo natural del tiempo por horarios de trabajo y calendario escolar.

Y nosotros ingresamos a la escuela del barrio, portando rostros y apellidos, sin idioma del cual avergonzarnos, con el castellano como primera y única lengua. Sin historia, sin memoria.

Hablo de Puel Mapu y de la historia de mi familia que es la historia de muchas familias y que explica la pérdida de nuestro idioma como primera lengua, en la mayoría de mi generación. Hablo de una lengua milenaria y la ignorancia de los hombres que proyectaron un país sobre unterritorio pleno de nombres, fuerzas y significados; silenciándolo. Hablo de lo que nos perdimos. Todos.

Todos los que nacimos sin saber el nombre de cada planta, cada piedra y cada pájaro de esta tierra.

Yo desperté en el medio de un lago, a boqueadas intenté decir gracias y no supe las palabras. No me habían sido dadas. Encontré en la poesía en "castilla" la posibilidad de expresar algo de la profundidad que me inundaba. Y la nostalgia de dios, es decir, de una cosmovisión, me llevó por el camino a recuperar su idioma.

Cuando se cumplieron los 500 años del desencuentro, empezamos a aparecer de entre las matas y cada vez fuimos más regresando a nuestro origen. Haciéndonos visibles. Mapuche ta iñche fuimos diciendo para reconocernos y reparar un poco el daño que nos hicieron.

Within our community, the politics of shame wreaked havoc. Mapuzungun became a stigma, the mark of inferiority of those admitted by force to the capitalist system as cheap labor.

Perhaps the elders made a decision to stop teaching it. Could they get together? Did they speak in Mapuzungun of the future? Maybe they simply went silent, determining their knowledge to no longer suffice, that the saplings could manage better without them in this new world of constant threats, stigmas, accusations, smirks.

Mapuzungun was the language of conversation of the elders, the language for summoning the elements in the intimacy of dawn. The language of defense. Of silence. The city offered work and study to the saplings. Our parents arrived monolingual, without ngillatun, without Mapuzungun, exchanging the natural cycle of time for work hours and school calendars.

And we entered local schools, bearing our faces and surnames, without any language for which to feel ashamed, with Spanish as our one and only tongue, without history or memory.

I'm talking about Puel Mapu and the history of my family, which is the history of so many families, and which explains the loss of our language as mother tongue by the majority of my generation. I'm talking about an ancient language and the ignorance of men who mapped a country over a territory full of names, elements, and meanings, silencing it. I'm talking about what we lost. All of us.

All of us who were born without knowing the names of every plant, every stone, and every bird of this land.

I woke in the middle of a lake. In gasps I tried to give thanks but didn't know the words. They hadn't been taught to me. I found in poetry in Spanish the possibility to express something of the profundity that flooded me. And god's nostalgia, which is to say a cosmovision, carried me down the path to recovering his language.

On the 500th birthday of the discord, we began to emerge from the brush, and with each step we returned closer to our roots, making ourselves visible. We'd say Mapuche ta iñche to recognize ourselves and repair the damage they'd done to us but by bit.

El mapudungun es el idioma de recuperación del orgullo, el idioma de la reconstrucción de la memoria.

Las condiciones de enseñanza y aprendizaje de nuestro idioma son cada vez más dificultosas en la medida en que pasa el tiempo y van muriendo los ancianos portadores del conocimiento. Urge una política lingüística por parte del estado que aporte con recursos y acelere el proceso de recuperación del idioma. Proceso de recuperación en el que además de la oralidad, adoptamos la escritura y pensamos métodos de enseñanza y aprendizaje de nuestro idioma como segunda lengua.

Ir aprendiéndolo es un camino de asombro. A mí se me agranda el corazón cada vez que explico que en el mapuzungun, además del singular y el plural, existe el pronombre dual: iñchiu significa "nosotros dos," eymu significa "ustedes dos" y fey engü significa "ellos dos." El par es el equilibrio en nuestra cosmovisión.

Aprendo y practico las palabras para convocar y propiciar las fuerzas. Vivo en la ciudad donde ejerzo mi profesión y en la que me cuesta no sucumbir al individualismo occidental: Kishungenelan es la enseñanza que nos dejan los ancianos.

Pienso en castellano y escribo, luego traduzco con torpeza al idioma que me seduce con su inmensidad y profundidad azul.

Mapuzungun is the language of the recovery of pride, the language of the reconstruction of memory.

The conditions for teaching and learning our language are ever more difficult because as time passes, the elder bearing our knowledge die. The federal government should push a linguistic politics to accelerate and support with resources the process of recovery of our language. A process of recovery to include not only orality, but also our adoption of writing and of the creation of methods for teaching and learning our language as a second language.

To learn it is to travel a path of amazements. My heart swells each time I explain that in Mapuzungun, besides the singular and plural, there exist the dual pronouns iñchiu, meaning "we two," eymu, meaning "you two," and fey engü, meaning "them two." Pairs give balance to our cosmovision.

I learn and practice the words for summoning and serving the elements. I live in the city, where I have a profession and struggle not to succumb to western individualism: Kishungenelan is the teaching given us by the elders.

I think and write in Spanish, and later translate it clumsily into the language that seduces me with its immense, deep blue.

Notes:

"ngellípun üngümafiel ti colectivo": Translation by Víctor Cifuentes, published in "La memoria iluminada: poesía mapuche contemporánea" Edición de Jaime Luis Huenún, versión mapuchezüngun de Víctor Cifuentes, CEDMA Ediciones de la Diputación de Málaga, 2007.

Glossary

Che: people

Choike: ostrich

Chulengo: a guanaco foal

Copawe: Copawe, or Copahue, is a stratovolcano in the Andes on the border between Argentina and Chile

Kalfuwenufuchá kalfuwenukushe: this is Liliana's Mapuche divine invocation, and it literally translates as Elders of the Blue Above

Ka Mapu: distant land

Ka mollfunche: foreign people, of a different blood

Kishungenelan: I am not guided by myself alone

Konas: warriors

Manzana Mapu: This refers to the swath of Patagonia containing vast apple orchards, which featured prominently in the Mapuche diet of the region and were termed manzanache or manzaneros by the Mapuche.

Mapu: land

Mapuche ta iñche: I am Mapuche

Ngillatun: propitiatory ritual

Orkeke and Casimiro: Orkeke (c.1810-1884) was a Tehuelche cacique in territorial Argentina who led his people up and down Route 40 before being captured by the Argentine army for resisting the state's authority and transferred to Buenos Aires, where he died. Of note he also willingly guided the British explorer George Chaworth Musters on his journey through Patagonia in the 1850s. Casimiro Biguá (1819-1874) was a Tehuelche cacique in territorial Argentina who on 3 November 1869 raised the Argentine flag. Of note, for his effort to recognize Argentine sovereignty over Tehuelche and Mapuche land, he had been named a Lieutenant Colonel of the Argentine Army by Argentine President Bartolomé Mitre on 5 July 1865.

Puel Mapu: land of the east, actually Argentina

Pu lamngen: my brothers and sisters

Tayüll: the sacred song of a family lineage

Trutruka: an indigenous horn of the Mapuche people.

Winka: strange, foreign, enemy

Zungun: speak, language

About the Author

A leading Mapuche poet, Liliana Ancalao was born in 1961 in what is today Argentina. Besides being an esteemed poet and oral historian, she also works with the Mapuche community group Ñamkulawen to advance Mapuche culture, including the reclamation of Mapuzungun. She has published the books of poetry *Tejido con lana cruda* and *Mujeres a la intemperie-pu zomo wekuntu mew*, as well as a book of essays and poetry titled *Resuello-neyen*. She has been widely anthologized both within and beyond Argentina in books on Mapuche poetry, Argentine poetry, and indigenous poetry, and her work has been translated in English and French. A retired literature teacher, she resides in Commodoro Rivadavia.

About the Translator

Seth Michelson is an award-winning poet, translator, and professor of poetry. He has published fourteen books of original poetry and poetry in translation, and he also edited the bilingual-Spanish poetry anthology *Dreaming America: Voices of Undocumented Youth in Maximum-Security Detention* (Settlement House, 2017), with all proceeds from its sale going to the incarcerated youth. He currently teaches the poetry of the Americas at Washington and Lee University, where he founded and directs the Center for Poetic Research.

About The Word Works

Since its founding in 1974, The Word Works has steadily published volumes of contemporary poetry and presented public programs. Its imprints include The Washington Prize, The Tenth Gate Prize, The Hilary Tham Capital Collection, and International Editions.

Monthly, The Word Works offers free literary programs in the Café Muse series at the Writers Center in Bethesda, MD, and each summer it holds free poetry programs in Washington, D.C.'s Rock Creek Park. Word Works programs have included "In the Shadow of the Capitol," a symposium and archival project on the African American intellectual community in segregated Washington, D.C.; the Gunston Arts Center Poetry Series; the Poet Editor panel discussions at The Writer's Center; Master Class workshops; and a writing retreat in Tuscany, Italy.

As a 501(c)3 organization, The Word Works has received awards from the National Endowment for the Arts, the National Endowment for the Humanities, the D.C. Commission on the Arts & Humanities, the Witter Bynner Foundation, Poets & Writers, The Writer's Center, Bell Atlantic, the David G. Taft Foundation, and others, including many generous private patrons.

It is a member of the Community of Literary Magazines and Presses and its books are distributed by Small Press Distribution.

wordworksbooks.org

OTHER WORD WORKS BOOKS

Annik Adey-Babinski, *Okay Cool No Smoking Love Pony*
Karren L. Alenier, *Wandering on the Outside*
Karren L. Alenier, ed., *Whose Woods These Are*
Karren L. Alenier & Miles David Moore, eds., *Winners: A Retrospective of the Washington Prize*
Christopher Bursk, ed., *Cool Fire*
Willa Carroll, *Nerve Chorus*
Grace Cavalieri, *Creature Comforts*
Abby Chew, *A Bear Approaches from the Sky*
Nadia Colburn, *The High Shelf*
Henry Crawford, *Binary Planet*
Barbara Goldberg, *Berta Broadfoot and Pepin the Short*
Akua Lezli Hope, *Them Gone*
Frannie Lindsay, *If Mercy*
Elaine Maggarrell, *The Madness of Chefs*
Marilyn McCabe, *Glass Factory*
Kevin McLellan, *Ornitheology*
JoAnne McFarland, *Identifying the Body*
Leslie McGrath, *Feminists Are Passing from Our Lives*
Ann Pelletier, *Letter That Never*
Ayaz Pirani, *Happy You Are Here*
W.T. Pfefferle, *My Coolest Shirt*
Jacklyn Potter, Dwaine Rieves, Gary Stein, eds., *Cabin Fever: Poets at Joaquin Miller's Cabin*
Robert Sargent, *Aspects of a Southern Story* & *A Woman from Memphis*
Julia Story, *Spinster for Hire*
Miles Waggener, *Superstition Freeway*
Fritz Ward, *Tsunami Diorama*
Camille-Yvette Welsh, *The Four Ugliest Children in Christendom*
Amber West, *Hen & God*
Maceo Whitaker, *Narco Farm*
Nancy White, ed., *Word for Word*

THE WASHINGTON PRIZE

Nathalie Anderson, *Following Fred Astaire*, 1998

Michael Atkinson, *One Hundred Children Waiting for a Train*, 2001

Molly Bashaw, *The Whole Field Still Moving Inside It*, 2013

Carrie Bennett, *biography of water*, 2004

Peter Blair, *Last Heat*, 1999

John Bradley, *Love-in-Idleness: The Poetry of Roberto Zingarello*, 1995, 2ND edition 2014

Christopher Bursk, *The Way Water Rubs Stone*, 1988

Richard Carr, *Ace*, 2008

Jamison Crabtree, *Rel[AM]ent*, 2014

Jessica Cuello, *Hunt*, 2016

Barbara Duffey, *Simple Machines*, 2015

B. K. Fischer, *St. Rage's Vault*, 2012

Linda Lee Harper, *Toward Desire*, 1995

Ann Rae Jonas, *A Diamond Is Hard but Not Tough*, 1997

Annie Kim, *Eros, Unbroken*, 2019

Susan Lewis, *Zoom*, 2017

Frannie Lindsay, *Mayweed*, 2009

Richard Lyons, *Fleur Carnivore*, 2005

Elaine Magarrell, *Blameless Lives*, 1991

Fred Marchant, *Tipping Point*, 1993, 2ND edition 2013

Nils Michals, *Gembox*, 2018

Ron Mohring, *Survivable World*, 2003

Barbara Moore, *Farewell to the Body*, 1990

Brad Richard, *Motion Studies*, 2010

Jay Rogoff, *The Cutoff*, 1994

Prartho Sereno, *Call from Paris*, 2007, 2ND edition 2013

Enid Shomer, *Stalking the Florida Panther*, 1987

John Surowiecki, *The Hat City After Men Stopped Wearing Hats*, 2006

Miles Waggener, *Phoenix Suites*, 2002

Charlotte Warren, *Gandhi's Lap*, 2000

Mike White, *How to Make a Bird with Two Hands*, 2011

Nancy White, *Sun, Moon, Salt*, 1992, 2ND edition 2010

George Young, *Spinoza's Mouse*, 1996

THE HILARY THAM CAPITAL COLLECTION

Nathalie Anderson, *Stain*

Mel Belin, *Flesh That Was Chrysalis*

Carrie Bennett, *The Land Is a Painted Thing*

Doris Brody, *Judging the Distance*

Sarah Browning, *Whiskey in the Garden of Eden*

Grace Cavalieri, *Pinecrest Rest Haven*

Cheryl Clarke, *By My Precise Haircut*

Christopher Conlon, *Gilbert and Garbo in Love* & *Mary Falls: Requiem for Mrs. Surratt*

Donna Denizé, *Broken Like Job*

W. Perry Epes, *Nothing Happened*

David Eye, *Seed*

Bernadette Geyer, *The Scabbard of Her Throat*

Elizabeth Gross, *this body / that lightning show*

Barbara G. S. Hagerty, *Twinzilla*

Lisa Hase-Jackson, *Flint & Fire*

James Hopkins, *Eight Pale Women*

Donald Illich, *Chance Bodies*

Brandon Johnson, *Love's Skin*

Thomas March, *Aftermath*

Marilyn McCabe, *Perpetual Motion*

Judith McCombs, *The Habit of Fire*

James McEwen, *Snake Country*

Miles David Moore, *The Bears of Paris* & *Rollercoaster*

Kathi Morrison-Taylor, *By the Nest*

Tera Vale Ragan, *Reading the Ground*

Michael Shaffner, *The Good Opinion of Squirrels*

Maria Terrone, *The Bodies We Were Loaned*

Hilary Tham, *Bad Names for Women* & *Counting*

Barbara Ungar, *Charlotte Brontë, You Ruined My Life* & *Immortal Medusa*

Jonathan Vaile, *Blue Cowboy*

Rosemary Winslow, *Green Bodies*

Kathleen Winter, *Transformer*

Michele Wolf, *Immersion*

Joe Zealberg, *Covalence*

About The Word Works

Since its founding in 1974, The Word Works has steadily published volumes of contemporary poetry and presented public programs. Its imprints include The Washington Prize, The Tenth Gate Prize, The Hilary Tham Capital Collection, and International Editions.

Monthly, The Word Works offers free literary programs in the Café Muse series at the Writers Center in Bethesda, MD, and each summer it holds free poetry programs in Washington, D.C.'s Rock Creek Park. Word Works programs have included "In the Shadow of the Capitol," a symposium and archival project on the African American intellectual community in segregated Washington, D.C.; the Gunston Arts Center Poetry Series; the Poet Editor panel discussions at The Writer's Center; Master Class workshops; and a writing retreat in Tuscany, Italy.

As a 501(c)3 organization, The Word Works has received awards from the National Endowment for the Arts, the National Endowment for the Humanities, the D.C. Commission on the Arts & Humanities, the Witter Bynner Foundation, Poets & Writers, The Writer's Center, Bell Atlantic, the David G. Taft Foundation, and others, including many generous private patrons.

It is a member of the Community of Literary Magazines and Presses and its books are distributed by Small Press Distribution.

wordworksbooks.org

OTHER WORD WORKS BOOKS

Annik Adey-Babinski, *Okay Cool No Smoking Love Pony*
Karren L. Alenier, *Wandering on the Outside*
Karren L. Alenier, ed., *Whose Woods These Are*
Karren L. Alenier & Miles David Moore, eds., *Winners: A Retrospective of the Washington Prize*
Christopher Bursk, ed., *Cool Fire*
Willa Carroll, *Nerve Chorus*
Grace Cavalieri, *Creature Comforts*
Abby Chew, *A Bear Approaches from the Sky*
Nadia Colburn, *The High Shelf*
Henry Crawford, *Binary Planet*
Barbara Goldberg, *Berta Broadfoot and Pepin the Short*
Akua Lezli Hope, *Them Gone*
Frannie Lindsay, *If Mercy*
Elaine Maggarrell, *The Madness of Chefs*
Marilyn McCabe, *Glass Factory*
Kevin McLellan, *Ornitheology*
JoAnne McFarland, *Identifying the Body*
Leslie McGrath, *Feminists Are Passing from Our Lives*
Ann Pelletier, *Letter That Never*
Ayaz Pirani, *Happy You Are Here*
W.T. Pfefferle, *My Coolest Shirt*
Jacklyn Potter, Dwaine Rieves, Gary Stein, eds., *Cabin Fever: Poets at Joaquin Miller's Cabin*
Robert Sargent, *Aspects of a Southern Story* & *A Woman from Memphis*
Julia Story, *Spinster for Hire*
Miles Waggener, *Superstition Freeway*
Fritz Ward, *Tsunami Diorama*
Camille-Yvette Welsh, *The Four Ugliest Children in Christendom*
Amber West, *Hen & God*
Maceo Whitaker, *Narco Farm*
Nancy White, ed., *Word for Word*

INTERNATIONAL EDITIONS

Kajal Ahmad (Alana Marie Levinson-LaBrosse, Mewan Nahro Said Sofi, and
    Darya Abdul-Karim Ali Najin, trans., with Barbara Goldberg), *Handful of Salt*
Liliana Ancalao (Seth Michelson, trans.), *Women of the Big Sky*
Keyne Cheshire (trans.), *Murder at Jagged Rock: A Tragedy by Sophocles*
Jeannette L. Clariond (Curtis Bauer, trans.), *Image of Absence*
Jean Cocteau (Mary-Sherman Willis, trans.), *Grace Notes*
Yoko Danno & James C. Hopkins, *The Blue Door*
Moshe Dor, Barbara Goldberg, Giora Leshem, eds., *The Stones Remember: Native Israeli Poets*
Moshe Dor (Barbara Goldberg, trans.), *Scorched by the Sun*
Laura Cesarco Eglin (Jesse Lee Kercheval and Catherine Jagoe,
    trans.), *Reborn in Ink*
Vladimir Levchev (Henry Taylor, trans.), *Black Book of the Endangered Species*
Marko Pogačar (Andrea Jurjević, trans.), *Dead Letter Office*
Lee Sang (Myong-Hee Kim, trans.) *Crow's Eye View: The Infamy of Lee Sang, Korean Poet*

THE TENTH GATE PRIZE

Jennifer Barber, *Works on Paper*, 2015
Christine Hamm, *Gorilla*, 2019
Lisa Lewis, *Taxonomy of the Missing*, 2017
Brad Richard, *Parasite Kingdom*, 2018
Roger Sedarat, *Haji As Puppet*, 2016
Lisa Sewell, *Impossible Object*, 2014

CPSIA information can be obtained
at www.ICGtesting.com
Printed in the USA
LVHW051508131222
735074LV00013B/475